Super Heroes Prayer Book

Copyright © 2016 by Christian Art Kids,
an imprint of Christian Art Publishers,
PO Box 1599, Vereeniging, 1930, RSA

359 Longview Drive, Bloomingdale, IL, 60108, USA

First edition 2016

Designed by Christian Art Kids

Illustrations by Joe Goode

Images used under license from Shutterstock.com

Scripture quotations are taken from the *Holy Bible*, New Living Translation®,
copyright © 1996, 2004, 2007, 2013 by Tyndale House Foundation. Used by
permission of Tyndale House Publishers, Inc., Carol Stream, Illinois 60188.
All rights reserved.

Scripture quotations are taken from the *Holy Bible*, Contemporary English Version®.
Copyright © 1995 by American Bible Society. All rights reserved.

Printed in China

ISBN 978-1-4321-1427-5

16 17 18 19 20 21 22 23 24 25 – 10 9 8 7 6 5 4 3 2 1

SUPER HEROES PRAYER BOOK

Written by Carolyn Larsen • Illustrated by Joe Goode

christian art kids

Contents

The World Is a Scary Place

Dear God,

I don't want anyone else to know but ...
I'm kind of scared. Stuff like wars,
bad storms and mean people scare me.
Help me to remember that You are in charge
so I don't have to be so scared.

Amen.

God is our refuge and strength,
always ready to help in times of trouble.

– PSALM 46:1 –

Dear God,

I have a big sports game coming up.
It's big because I'm going to be in a new
position, so I'm a bit nervous. I'm scared
that I won't do a good job and
will make us lose. Help me, God.
Help me to do my best.

Amen.

"Don't be afraid, for I am with you.
Don't be discouraged, for I am your God.
I will strengthen you and help you. I will hold
you up with My victorious right hand."

- ISAIAH 41:10 -

Moving Away

Dear God,

We're moving to a new town
and I'm scared. I like my friends
and I'm afraid it will be hard to make
friends in the new place. I hope I can
find friends who like the same things I like.
Will You help me, God? Thanks.

Amen.

Our help is from the LORD,
who made heaven and earth.

- PSALM 124:8 -

12

Yelling Is Scary

Dear God,

Mom and Dad yell at each other sometimes. I don't like it when they are angry. I'm scared that they might get a divorce. Then what will happen to me? Help them, God. Help them to talk and not yell.

Amen.

You will keep in perfect peace all who trust in You, all whose thoughts are fixed on You!

- ISAIAH 26:3 -

Secret Fears

Dear God,

Don't tell anyone this, OK? But I'm scared of the dark. When my room is dark I think there might be monsters under my bed or bad guys in the closet. Help me to remember that You are with me so I don't need to be scared.

Amen.

I lay down and slept, yet I woke up in safety, for the LORD was watching over me.

– PSALM 3:5 –

Scared of Everything

Dear God,

Super heroes aren't supposed to be scared but ...
I'm scared. I'm scared that I won't do well in school.
I'm scared that my friends won't like me. I'm scared
that I won't obey You. I'm tired of being scared.
Help me to trust You and not be scared.

Amen.

"Be strong and courageous!
Do not be afraid or discouraged.
For the LORD your God is with you
wherever you go."

- JOSHUA 1:9 -

15

Obeying When
I Don't Want To

Dear God,

Someone is always telling me things I have to do. When I get tired of obeying I get grumpy. That gets me into trouble. Help me to understand why obeying is important. Help me to be better about obeying You and my parents. I know it's the right thing to do. It just isn't always fun.

Amen.

The Lord says, "If you love Me, you will do what I have said, and My Father will love you. I will also love you and show you what I am like."
– JOHN 14:21 –

Secretly Disobeying

Dear God,

My parents tell me I have to obey them. Okay, fine. I do, but I'm only obeying on the outside. On the inside I'm screaming and complaining about it. It feels like I'm only pretending to obey. Please help me with how I feel about this. Help me to obey with all my heart.

Amen.

Children, obey your parents because you belong to the Lord, for this is the right thing to do.

- EPHESIANS 6:1 -

Rules Have a Reason

Dear God,

Mom and Dad have rules that I must obey.
Sometimes I think these things are fun,
like jumping on the bed. Help me to remember
that their rules help keep me safe.
It will make it easier to obey.

Amen.

Children, always obey your parents,
for this pleases the Lord.

- COLOSSIANS 3:20 -

Learning from Obeying

Dear God,

My mom and dad say that super heroes obey rules and laws. They say that learning to obey will help me to be a better person. I want to be the best super hero ever, so please help me to learn important stuff every time I obey.

Amen.

God blesses those people who refuse evil advice and won't follow sinners or join in sneering at God. Instead, the Law of the LORD makes them happy, and they think about it day and night.

– PSALM 1:1-2 –

Obeying with My Mouth

Dear God,

It is hard to obey with my mouth. I'm sorry that I talk back to Mom and Dad sometimes. I know I'm not supposed to ... I always get into trouble for it. Please help me to control my words. Help me to be respectful to Mom and Dad in what I say.

Amen.

You must all be quick to listen, slow to speak, and slow to get angry.

– JAMES 1:19 –

Why Obeying Is Important

Dear God,

Obeying is hard sometimes. That's because I forget that disobeying my parents, teachers and especially You is actually sin. That's a big deal. Help me to remember that disobeying just because I don't feel like obeying is wrong. I don't want to sin on purpose. Please help me.

Amen.

You used to be like people living in the dark, but now you are people of the light because you belong to the Lord. So act like people of the light and make your light shine. Be good and honest and truthful.

- EPHESIANS 5:8-9 -

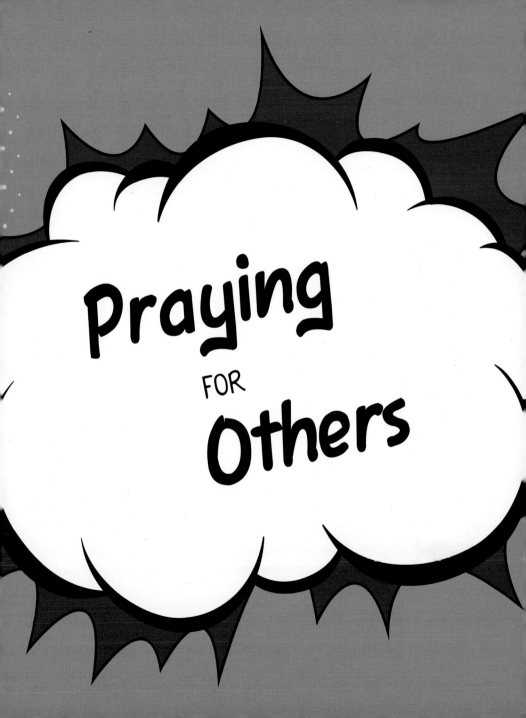

Best Friends in the World

Dear God,

I have some pretty cool friends.
We all like playing games ... like super heroes.
We play sports, and lots of other games.
Thank You for giving me good friends
who care about me. Help me to be
a good friend to them, too.

Amen.

Give thanks to the LORD, for He is good!
His faithful love endures forever.

- 1 CHRONICLES 16:34 -

My Friend Needs You

Dear God,

I have an awesome friend. I care about him a lot. But his family doesn't go to church, so he doesn't know anything about You. I want him to know that You love him. Help me to find the right way and right time to tell him about You.

Amen.

The LORD said, "If I tell you to go and speak to someone, then go! And when I tell you what to say, don't leave out a word! I promise to be with you and keep you safe, so don't be afraid."

– JEREMIAH 1:7-8 –

27

My Friend Is Sick

Dear God,

My friend is sick. I wish I could help him.
Super heroes are supposed to help people. Mom says
the best way to help my friend is to pray for him.
She says to ask You to help him get better.
So, please God, help my friend get well.

Amen.

The Lord says, "Ask, and you will
receive. Search, and you will find. Knock,
and the door will be opened for you."

– MATTHEW 7:7 –

When Bad Things Happen

Dear God,

There are big storms wrecking things in some places. In other places there's fighting where even little kids get hurt. It's scary for me to hear about these things, but it must be even scarier for the people going through them. Please help them, God. Protect them and help them.

Amen.

The LORD is a shelter for the oppressed,
a refuge in times of trouble.

- PSALM 9:9 -

A Lonely Guy

Dear God,

This guy at my school doesn't have friends.
He's different from the rest of us so he doesn't fit in.
He's always by himself so he must be pretty lonely.
I pray for him to be able to make friends. Help me
to be brave enough to be his first friend.

Amen.

If you love only those people who love you,
will God reward you for that? Even tax
collectors love their friends.

– MATTHEW 5:46 –

Help My Friend

Dear God,

When I pretend to be a super hero, I pretend to help people who have problems. One of my friends has a problem. I can be his friend, but I can't make his problem go away. That's why I'm asking You to please help him.

Amen.

Where will I find help?
It will come from the LORD,
who created the heavens and the earth.

- PSALM 121:1-2 -

Learning from What I Don't Like to Do

Dear God,

I don't always like to read. I like to run and jump and stuff like that. But, I want to know You better so I need to read my Bible. I'm going to try to read it every day. Please help me to understand it and to remember what I read.

Amen.

When I discovered Your words, I devoured them. They are my joy and my heart's delight.

– JEREMIAH 15:16 –

Forgiveness Is a Good Thing

Dear God,

When I sin ... do something wrong, mean, unkind or selfish ... then it's like a roadblock to knowing You better. Thank You so much that when I ask You to forgive my sins, that roadblock is taken down.
You are awesome.

Amen.

If we confess our sins to God, He can always be trusted to forgive us and take our sins away.

– 1 John 1:9 –

Practice Makes Perfect

Dear God,

I like to play sports. The more I play, the better I get. It's the same with other stuff ... the more I do something, the better I get. That's also true about knowing You ... the more I read Your Word and pray, the better I know You. Help me to remember that.

Amen.

Don't be like the people of this world, but let God change the way you think. Then you will know how to do everything that is good and pleasing to Him.

- ROMANS 12:2 -

Private Chats

Dear God,

I think it's really awesome that I can talk with You whenever I want. I don't have to use fancy words. I can just tell You what I'm thinking and feeling. I know that You want to know that stuff because You love me. I like that. Thank You.

Amen.

The LORD is close to all who call on Him, yes, to all who call on Him in truth.

– PSALM 145:18 –

I Don't Get It

Dear God,

I'm just a kid so how can I know You? Grown-ups are better at it, I think. Help me to learn to know You one step at a time. Help me to learn to obey You one thing at a time. Help me to learn to love You because I know You love me.

Amen.

I am sure that nothing can separate us from God's love.

– ROMANS 8:38 –

Thinking Things Through

Dear God,

Sometimes I do things without really thinking about what I'm doing. I guess that's when I make bad choices. That's when I sin. God, please guide my choices. Help me to remember to stop and think before I do stuff. Help me to think about obeying You.

Amen.

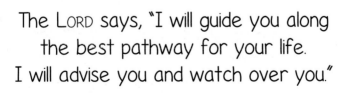

The LORD says, "I will guide you along
the best pathway for your life.
I will advise you and watch over you."

- PSALM 32:8 -

My Mom and Dad

Dear God,

My mom and dad are pretty awesome. It must be hard to go to work and then take care of all the stuff at home. But they still make time to play with me and read to me. They pray with me and teach me about You. Take care of them, please.

Amen.

As soon as I pray, You answer me; You encourage me by giving me strength.

- PSALM 138:3 -

My Brother

Dear God,

Okay, so sometimes it's hard to have brothers.
My brother picks on me. He's mean sometimes.
But then sometimes he is fun and he
plays with me and teaches me stuff.
I love my brother. Thank You for
giving me my brother.

Amen.

Most important of all, continue to show deep love
for each other, for love covers a multitude of sins.

- 1 PETER 4:8 -

My Sister

Dear God,

I have a sister. I like to make her laugh. It's so much fun to teach her stuff. Even if she doesn't like super heroes, we can find other stuff to do. Help me to be a good brother and to watch out for her and help her.

Amen.

No one has ever seen God. But if we love each other, God lives in us, and His love is truly in our hearts.

- 1 JOHN 4:12 -

The Best Grandparents Ever

Dear God,

Thank You so much for my grandma and grandpa. They love me so much. I like to visit them. We have such fun together. I love them a lot. Take care of them, God.

Amen.

Grandparents are proud of their grandchildren, and children should be proud of their parents.

- PROVERBS 17:6 -

Being in a Family

Dear God,

I can be pretty grumpy sometimes. At other times I am mean to my brother. I don't always obey Mom and Dad. I don't know why I act like that. Please help me to be nicer. Help me to get over being grumpy so I can be easier to get along with.

Amen.

"Do to others whatever you would like them to do to you."

– MATTHEW 7:12 –

Favorite Night

Dear God,

IT'S FAMILY NIGHT! My favorite night of the whole week. Mom and Dad are both home. We eat together and talk and laugh. Then sometimes we play games or watch movies. I love my family. It's fun to be together.

Amen.

The Lord says, "So now I am giving you a new commandment: Love each other. Just as I have loved you, you should love each other."

- JOHN 13:34 -

Why Do People Get Sick?

Dear God,

I know that sometimes people get sick.
I know that people die. I wish this didn't
have to happen. Help me to understand
why You don't just make everyone better.
Help me to trust You with my family.

Amen.

With all your heart you must
trust the LORD and not your own judgment.

- PROVERBS 3:5 -

Bad Things

Dear God,

There was a really bad storm and lots of people got hurt. Lots of homes were wrecked. I don't understand why You let those kinds of things happen, but I know You care. Please help them, God. Help them to feel better. Help them to not be scared. Please take care of them.

Amen.

The faithful love of the LORD never ends! His mercies never cease.

- LAMENTATIONS 3:22 -

Why Don't You Just Fix Things?

Dear God,

I don't get why You don't just fix all the things that hurt people. Someone said to me that people make choices that cause bad things to happen. That makes You sad for them, but I know You are always with people who are sad. That's good. Please stay close to them, God.

Amen.

Come close to God, and God will come close to You.

- JAMES 4:8 -

I Miss My Friend

Dear God,

Why did my friend have to move away? We had so much fun playing 'cause we like the same things. He was the best at being a super hero with me. I miss him. Please help me to find another friend who likes the same things I do. Help my friend to find new friends, too.

Amen.

Your thoughts are far beyond my understanding, much more than I could ever imagine.

- PSALM 139:17 -

God's Love

Dear God,

I can't believe how much You love me. You love me so much that You sent Jesus to die for my sins. Jesus loves me so much that He came to earth! I don't understand it, but I'm really glad that You love me that much!

Amen.

God loved the people of this world so much that He gave His only Son, so that everyone who has faith in Him will have eternal life and never really die.

– JOHN 3:16 –

Things God Thought Of

Dear God,

How did You think of making the earth go round so that the sun comes up and goes down? How did You think of seasons changing so it's hot and cold … but some places are always hot or cold? I don't know how You did it, but I think it's awesome!

Amen.

Because of our faith,
we know that the world was made at
God's command. We also know that what can
be seen was made out of what cannot be seen.

- HEBREWS 11:3 -

When I Talk Back

Dear God,

Sometimes when Mom tells me to do something or punishes me, I say something mean back to her. I don't know why I do that. It just gets me into more trouble. I don't mean to be disrespectful. It just happens. Will You please help me to stop talking back? Thank You.

Amen.

The tongue is like a spark. It is an evil power that dirties the rest of the body and sets a person's entire life on fire.

- JAMES 3:6 -

Salt and Light

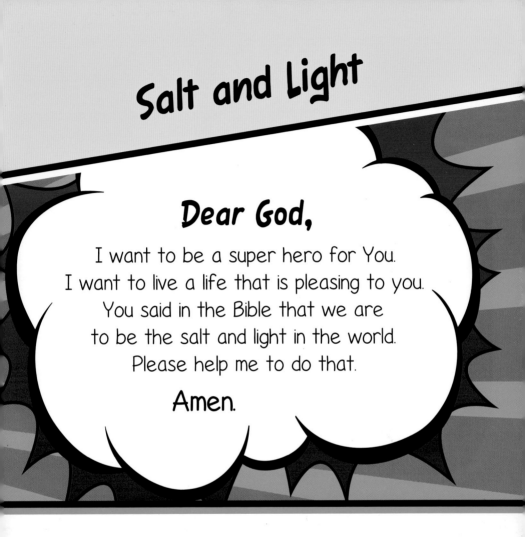

Dear God,

I want to be a super hero for You.
I want to live a life that is pleasing to you.
You said in the Bible that we are
to be the salt and light in the world.
Please help me to do that.

Amen.

Honesty guides good people;
dishonesty destroys treacherous people.

- PROVERBS 11:3 -

Forgive Me?

Dear God,

I mess up a lot. It's not on purpose, but I guess I just don't think sometimes before I do things or say things. I'm really sorry. Will You forgive me and help me to do better? It means a lot to know that You will. Thank You.

Amen.

The LORD says, "Though your sins are like scarlet, I will make them as white as snow. Though they are red like crimson, I will make them as white as wool."

– ISAIAH 1:18 –

60

Dump the Grump

Dear God,

Sometimes I feel grumpy. I say some mean things to just about everyone who tries to talk to me. I don't know why I get like this, but I know that it hurts people's feelings. I'm really sorry. Help me to be nicer, please.

Amen.

Love is kind and patient, never jealous, boastful, proud, or rude. Love isn't selfish or quick tempered. It doesn't keep a record of wrongs that others do.

- 1 CORINTHIANS 13:4-5 -

Fighting with My Brother

Dear God,

When I'm playing with something, my brother messes it u
When my friends come over, he won't leave us alone.
He gets me into trouble with Mom and Dad. Mom says
we should play together like friends, but he makes
me cross sometimes. Help me to get on with
my brother and be nicer to him.

Amen.

Don't sin by letting anger control you.
Don't let the sun go down while you are still angry.

- EPHESIANS 4:26 -

Telling Lies

Dear God,

I told a lie. I said I didn't know who caused the problem. I did it, but I lied so that I wouldn't get into trouble. I don't like how I feel when I lie. I know You are disappointed in me. Please forgive me. Help me to be completely honest.

Amen.

You must be truthful with each other.

- ZECHARIAH 8:16 -

Praise for Power

Dear God,

I see Your power everywhere I look. The crashing of waterfalls says You are strong. Ocean waves slamming into the shore shout power. I see Your might when thunder booms and lightning lights up the sky. I see Your power in a million ways. Thank You for being so powerful!

Amen.

You are worthy, O Lord our God, to receive glory and honor and power. For You created all things, and they exist because You created what You pleased.

– REVELATION 4:11 –

Praise for Love

Dear God,

Thank You for loving me so much. You love me even when I'm not being kind or helpful. You love me when I'm grumpy. You love me when I'm scared. You love me when I'm happy. You love me, no matter what. That's pretty awesome!

Amen.

We know how much God loves us,
and we have put our trust in His love. God is love,
and all who live in love live in God, and God lives in them.

- 1 JOHN 4:16 -

Praise for Creation

Dear God,

You made an awesome world! How did You think of so many different things? Things like mountains and oceans and waterfalls and deserts and canyons and forests and stars and the moon and the sun and trees and flowers and grass. It's all so cool!

Amen.

In the beginning God created the heavens and the earth.

- GENESIS 1:1 -

Praise for God's Plan

Dear God,

Thank You that I can know You. Was it hard to let Jesus come when You knew that bad things would happen to Him? That was an important part of the plan for people to be able to know You. It shows me that You love us a lot. You love ME a lot!

Amen.

God showed how much He loved us by having Christ die for us, even though we were sinful.

- ROMANS 5:8 -

Praise for Forgiveness

Dear God,

I am really thankful that You forgive me when I mess up because I mess up a lot. It's really cool that You give me a chance to do better. You must love me a lot to keep forgiving me and giving me more chances. That is so cool. You are awesome!

Amen.

The LORD says, "I will forgive their wickedness, and I will never again remember their sins."

- HEBREWS 8:12 -

Praise for Cool Things

Dear God,

Thank You for all the cool things You do for me.
Grown-ups call them blessings. I just think they
are cool things. Things like taking care of me,
loving me, giving me friends and giving me
my own family. Really cool things. Thank You.

Amen.

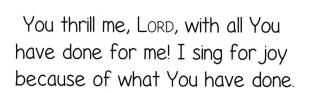

You thrill me, LORD, with all You
have done for me! I sing for joy
because of what You have done.

- PSALM 92:4 -

I'm Sad about My Pet

Dear God,

My pet died, and I feel really sad. I loved my pet a lot. I don't know if I'll get to see them again. My heart is sore. Please help me to feel better soon.

Amen.

He heals the brokenhearted and bandages their wounds.

- PSALM 147:3 -

Learning New Things

Dear God,

Sometimes school is boring and I don't want to do all the things my teacher says I must do. Please help me to remember that learning new things is cool and that school is good for me.

Amen.

God our Father loves us. He is kind and has given us eternal comfort and a wonderful hope.

- 2 THESSALONIANS 2:16 -

Sad for What I Want

Dear God,

I saw an awesome new toy. I asked Mom and Dad to get it for me, but they said no because I have tons of toys. That makes me sad. Would You help me to be thankful for what I have instead of sad for what I don't have?

Amen.

Let the peace that comes from Christ control your thoughts. And be grateful.

- COLOSSIANS 3:15 -

Feeling Bad for People Who Don't Know God

Dear God,

I am sad for kids who don't know about You. Some parents don't take their kids to church because they don't know You either. Please send people to tell these kids about You. Please show me how I can do my part.

Amen.

"Go into all the world and preach the Good News to everyone."

— MARK 16:15 —

My Heart Hurts

Dear God,

My heart is hurting pretty bad. My favorite uncle died. We did lots of fun things together. Why do people have to die? I loved him a lot. I'm going to miss him. Help me, God. This hurts a lot.

Amen.

Give all your worries and cares to God,
for He cares about you.

— 1 PETER 5:7 —

Help When I Need It

Dear God,

You always help me when I'm sad. Thank You for caring when I'm sad. Thank You for helping me to remember that You love me a lot. Thank You for reminding me that whatever I'm sad about will get better if I can hang in there for a while.

Amen.

Suffering helps us to endure.
And endurance builds character, which gives us a hope that will never disappoint us.
All of this happens because God has given us the Holy Spirit, who fills our hearts with His love.

- ROMANS 5:3-5 -

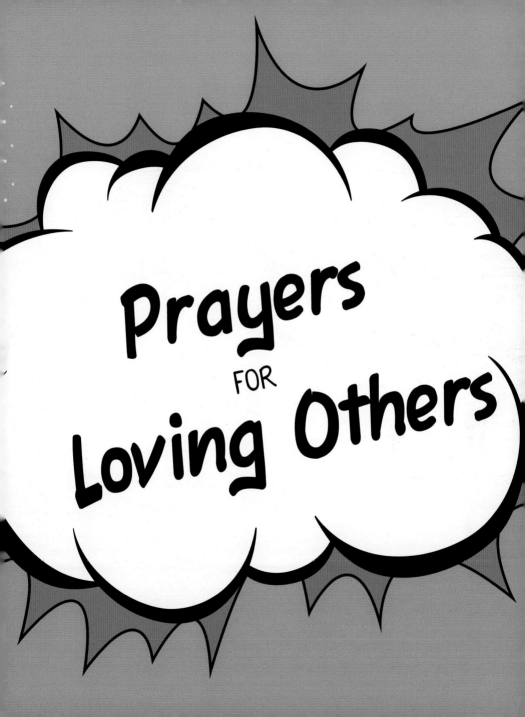

Mom and Dad

Dear God,

Mom and Dad love me. They take me to fun places. They take care of me and make sure that I have food and clothes and a home to live in. They teach me about You and pray with me and read the Bible with me. I love my mom and dad!

Amen.

Give thanks to the LORD and proclaim His greatness. Let the whole world know what He has done.

- 1 CHRONICLES 16:8 -

Some People Are Hard to Love

Dear God,

Some guys are just mean. There's this guy who picks on me and pushes me around sometimes. I know I'm supposed to love him like You say, but I'm going to need Your help with this. I can't find anything about him to like, never mind love. Help me, please.

Amen.

The Lord says, "Your love for one another will prove to the world that you are My disciples."

- JOHN 13:35 -

Tough Guys DO Love

Dear God,

I'm tough ... a super hero.
I don't want to be all mushy and soft. But,
Your Word tells me that I should love other people.
That doesn't sound very tough. But I know You
are super strong and powerful and You love,
so I know it's okay for me to love, too.

Amen.

Jesus says,
"Love your neighbor as yourself."

- MATTHEW 19:19 -

Loving My Buddies

Dear God,

I have some good friends. We have a great time together. We like to play the same sports. We laugh at the same kinds of things. They are a lot of fun. I'm really thankful for my buddies. Help me to be a good friend to them.

Amen.

God Himself has taught you to love one another.

- 1 THESSALONIANS 4:9 -

Loving Those Who Are Different

Dear God,

It's pretty easy to love my family and friends. But there are other people who need to be loved, too. People who are different from me ... speak another language or dress differently ... kind of scare me. I'm scared to even talk to them. God, help me to love them. Please show me how.

Amen.

The Lord says, "You have heard the law that says, 'Love your neighbor' and hate your enemy. But I say, love your enemies! Pray for those who persecute you!"

– MATTHEW 5:43-44 –

People Who Need Love

Dear God,

I've been hearing about people in other countries. Things are kind of tough for them. They have trouble growing food. They don't have clean water to drink. They get sick a lot. I know You love them, God. Please help them.

Amen.

The poor and the homeless won't always be forgotten and without hope.

- PSALM 9:18 -

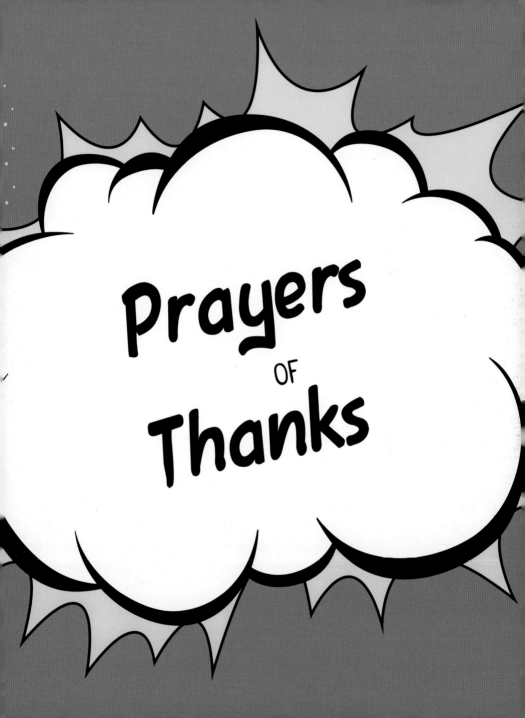

Thank You for Saving Me

Dear God,

Thank You for making a way for me to know You. It's really cool that You love me that much. Thank You for teaching me how to be a better person when I live for You. Thank You for making a place for me to live in heaven.

Amen.

Our LORD, let Your worshipers rejoice and be glad. They love You for saving them, so let them always say, "The LORD is wonderful!"

- PSALM 40:16 -

Thank You for Muscles and Energy

Dear God,

Thank You for giving me muscles and energy. I love that I can run and play with my friends. I think it's really cool that I grow bigger and stronger every year. I can do harder things in sports and run faster and jump higher. Thank You for helping me to grow!

Amen.

Give thanks for everything to God the Father in the name of our Lord Jesus Christ.

- EPHESIANS 5:20 -

Thank You for Sport

Dear God,

I love playing sport. I'm pretty good, too.
Thank You for thinking of sport. It's cool to be a part
of a team. It's fun to practice and know that I'm
getting better and better. It's fun to win. It's hard
to lose, but I learn good lessons from that.
Thank You for everything about sport!

Amen.

Be thankful and praise the LORD
as you enter His temple.

- PSALM 100:4 -

Thank You for My Teachers

Dear God,

Thank You for my teachers. I know they work hard and that I don't always pay attention when they're talking. Thank You for making them patient and kind.

Amen.

It is good to proclaim Your unfailing love in the morning, Your faithfulness in the evening.

– PSALM 92:2 –

93

Thank You for Ways I Can Help

Dear God,

I feel bad for kids who have lost their homes and stuff storms. Thank You for showing me ways I can help them Thank You for organizations that raise money to help them. I'm glad that I can have a part in it.

Amen.

Use your whole body as an instrument to do what is right for the glory of God.

- ROMANS 6:13 -

Thank You for Everything

Dear God,

Thank You for everything. Thank You for
the world You made. Thank You for sunshine.
Thank You for snow. Thank You for rivers and lakes.
Thank You for dogs and cats. Thank You for friends
and family. Thank You for ... You. Just, thank You.

Amen.

Whatever happens, keep
thanking God because of Jesus Christ.
This is what God wants you to do.

- 1 THESSALONIANS 5:18 -

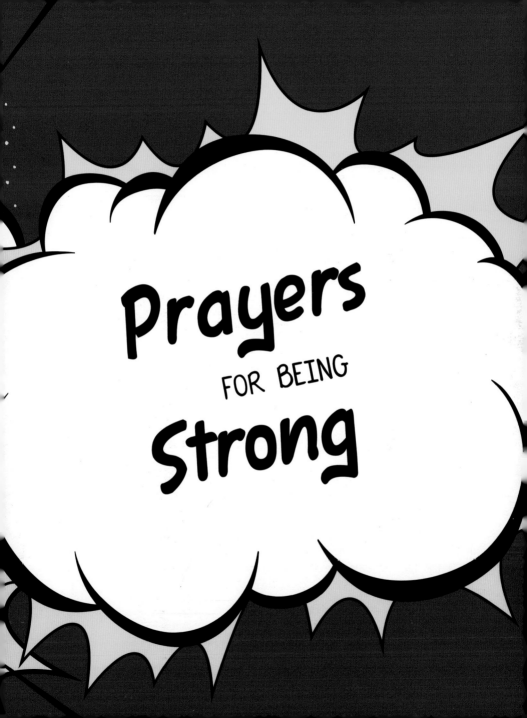

Growing Up and Getting Strong

Dear God,

I'm growing up and getting stronger every day. Thank You for helping me to do that. Thank You for good food that helps my body to grow stronger. Thank You for good sleep. Thank You for how You made me so that every day I grow. Help me to use my strength to serve You.

Amen.

I can do everything through Christ, who gives me strength.

- PHILIPPIANS 4:13 -

Being Strong
When I Don't Want to Be

Dear God,

Sometimes when bad things happen I don't want to be strong. I want to cry and pout. But that's not a big guy thing to do, so I try to be strong. It's hard, though. I trust You to take care of me, so please help me to be strong even when it's hard.

Amen.

The joy of the LORD is your strength!

- NEHEMIAH 8:10 -

Being Strong against a Bully

Dear God,

I need help being strong. There's this guy at school that pushes me around. He makes fun of me in front of other guys. I don't know why he's so mean to me, but it isn't fun. Help me to be strong and to stand up to him, but also to show Your love to him.

Amen.

He gives power to the weak
and strength to the powerless.

- ISAIAH 40:29 -

Strong Enough to Obey

Dear God,

Sometimes obeying is no fun. It feels like someone is always telling me stuff I have to do or stuff I can't do. I need strength from You to be good at obeying, because I don't do so well on my own. Help me, please.

Amen.

People who accept discipline are on the pathway to life, but those who ignore correction will go astray.

- PROVERBS 10:17 -

Strong When I'm Sad

Dear God,

The hardest kind of strength is when I have to be strong because something is making me sad. When I'm sad and start to feel down, it's hard to be strong. Please help me to know that You're with me when I'm sad. Help me to be strong.

Amen.

All praise to God, the Father of our Lord Jesus Christ. God is our merciful Father and the source of all comfort.

- 2 CORINTHIANS 1:3 -

Being Strong When I'm Scared

Dear God,

Sometimes I get scared about stuff. That's when I need to be strong. Help me to remember that You're in control. You know what's going on and nothing surprises You. I don't need to be scared. You'll take care of me. Help my faith to be strong.

Amen.

You go before me and follow me. You place Your hand of blessing on my head. Such knowledge is too wonderful for me, too great for me to understand!

– PSALM 139:5-6 –

103

Honesty Is the Best Policy

Dear God,

Help me to be honest with my friends. Sometimes I go along with whatever they want to do. That gets me into trouble if they do things I know aren't right. Help me to be honest and just say, "I don't think we should do that." Maybe they won't do it either then. That's helping them!

Amen.

The Lord says, "If you are faithful in little things, you will be faithful in large ones. But if you are dishonest in little things, you won't be honest with greater responsibilities."
- LUKE 16:10 -

Good Friends Are Loyal

Dear God,

I want to be the kind of guy who sticks by my friends, no matter what. Help me to be super-hero loyal so that, if I hear someone saying mean things about my friends, I can stick up for them. That's kind of scary, but it's what true friends do. Help me be that kind of friend.

Amen.

A friend is always loyal,
and a brother is born to help in time of need.

- PROVERBS 17:17 -

When My Friend's in Trouble

Dear God,

My friend has trouble at home. Sometimes he comes to my house just to get away. I don't know what to do except to ask You to help him. Help me to be a good friend and to help him through these times. Please help him.

Amen.

Love never gives up, never loses faith, is always hopeful, and endures through every circumstance.

- 1 CORINTHIANS 13:7 -

Disagreements

Dear God,

There are times when I get into an argument with a friend. I don't like it when this happens. Please help me to say I'm sorry so we can be friends again.

Amen.

Shout praises to the LORD!
With all my heart I will thank
the LORD when His people meet.

- PSALM 111:1 -

No Jealousy

Dear God,

I have a friend who is an awesome sports player. I wish I were as good as he is. Help me, God, to not be jealous of how good he is. Help me to cheer for him and celebrate with him when he has a good game. That's what a friend should do.

Amen.

Pride leads to destruction;
humility leads to honor.

– PROVERBS 18:12 –

New Friends

Dear God,

There is a new guy in school. He doesn't have any friends. He must be lonely, so please give me the courage to talk to him and to be his friend. Then I can introduce him to all of my friends, too!

Amen.

The whole law can be summed up in this one command: "Love your neighbor as yourself."

- GALATIANS 5:14 -

About Sin

Dear God,

Sin is when I'm unkind or don't play fair or am mean to my brother. It's when I disobey or complain about my chores. Would You help me to pay attention to when I sin? Then I can confess it and ask You to help me not to do that thing anymore.

Amen.

Everyone has sinned; we all fall short of God's glorious standard.

- ROMANS 3:23 -

I Did It Again

Dear God,

I try to obey my parents, but sometimes I get stubborn or grumpy and then I disobey. I tell them I'm sorry. I tell You I'm sorry. I ask for help to do better … but I end up doing it again. I really am sorry. Please help me to do better.

Amen.

Finally, I confessed all my sins to You and stopped trying to hide my guilt. I said to myself, "I will confess my rebellion to the LORD." And You forgave me! All my guilt is gone.

– PSALM 32:5 –

The Hardest Thing

Dear God,

My sister is annoying. She wants to play with me, but she can't play the cool stuff I like to play. She messes up my stuff. I'm not very nice to her sometimes. In fact, I'm mean. I need Your help to be kind and to teach her things so that we can play together.

Amen.

Be kind and merciful,
and forgive others, just as God
forgave you because of Christ.

- EPHESIANS 4:32 -

Thinking about Others

Dear God,

I'm pretty selfish. I want my parents to buy me stuff. I want my friends to play what I want to play. I just think about me. A lot of kids don't have homes or toys or even food. I'm sorry I'm so selfish. Forget my "I wants" and help those kids, please.

Amen.

Jesus says, "You must be compassionate, just as your Father is compassionate."

LUKE 6:36

Being Unkind

Dear God,

Please help me to be kinder to kids who aren't my friends. I guess I'm pretty mean to kids who don't seem to like the same stuff I like. I just kind of ignore kids who speak another language or are from another country. I'm sorry. Please forgive me and help me to be more kind.

Amen.

If you favor some people over others, you are committing a sin. You are guilty of breaking the law.

- JAMES 2:9 -

Ignoring God

Dear God,

I'm sorry for how I treat You sometimes.
I don't take time to read my Bible. I don't pay much
attention in church. I only pray when I want You to
do something. I'm sorry. The way I behave doesn't
show You how important You are to me.

Amen.

People who conceal their sins
will not prosper, but if they confess and
turn from them, they will receive mercy.

- PROVERBS 28:13 -

God Is Love

Dear God,

I know You love me a lot. You show me love all the time. Sometimes I don't pay attention to all You do for me. I'm sorry for that. I am so thankful for Your love. I love You, too.

Amen.

Anyone who does not love
does not know God, for God is love.

- 1 JOHN 4:8 -

God Is Forgiveness

Dear God,

I am super thankful for how You forgive me when I sin. I know I don't deserve Your forgiveness. But, You give it because You love me. Thank You for giving me second and third and hundreds of chances to do better.

Amen.

The Lord says, "If My own people will humbly pray and turn back to Me and stop sinning, then I will answer them from heaven. I will forgive them and make their land fertile once again."

- 2 CHRONICLES 7:14 -

123

God's Promises

Dear God,

Thank You for promising to help me and teach me how to live for You. Thank You for promising to always be with me. Thank You for promising heaven to me someday. I know You always keep Your promises. That's awesome.

Amen.

We must hold tightly to the hope that we say is ours. After all, we can trust the One who made the agreement with us.

- HEBREWS 10:23 -

God Is Always the Same

Dear God,

Thank You for never changing. You never get mad and stop talking to me like a friend might do. You never change the rules. You are always the same and I can count on Your love, no matter what. I like that.

Amen.

Jesus Christ is the same yesterday, today, and forever.

- HEBREWS 13:8 -

God Is Creative

Dear God,

You have the best ideas! Thank You for thinking of river and oceans. Thank You for thinking of sandy beaches and snowy winter mornings. Thank You for birds and bugs and pets and animals. You made something for everyone!

Amen.

Let everything that breathes sing praises to the LORD! Praise the LORD!

- PSALM 150:6 -

God Gives Blessings

Dear God,

It blows my mind to think about all Your blessings. You are so good to me. When I stop and think about it, every day in a million ways You bless me with super cool things. Thank You for loving me so much. Thank You for all the blessings You pile on me. You're awesome!

Amen.

The LORD has done amazing things for us! What joy!

- PSALM 92:4 -